I0795555

XTREME SPORTS

BASE JUMPING

BY RACHEL GRACK

EPIC

EPIC, AN IMPRINT OF BELLWETHER MEDIA BY FLUTTERBEE

EPIC

EPIC BOOKS are no ordinary books. They burst with intense action, high-speed heroics, and shadows of the unknown. Are you ready for an Epic adventure?

This edition first published in 2027 by Bellwether Media, Inc.

Text copyright © 2027 by Bellwether Media, Inc. All rights reserved. No part of this publication may be reproduced, stored in any retrieval system, or transmitted in any form or by any means, electronic, mechanical, photocopying, recording, or otherwise, without written permission of the publisher.

EPIC and associated logos are trademarks and/or registered trademarks of Bellwether Media, Inc. Bellwether Media is a division of FlutterBee Education Group.

For information regarding permission, write to Bellwether Media, Inc., Attention: Permissions Department, 3500 American Blvd W, Suite 150, Bloomington, MN 55431.

Library of Congress Cataloging-in-Publication Data is available at www.loc.gov or upon request from the publisher.

ISBN: 9798898800956 (hardcover)
ISBN: 9798898802196 (ebook)

Editor: Kieran Downs   Designer: Jeffrey Kollock

Printed in the United States of America, North Mankato, MN.

TABLE OF CONTENTS

FAST FREE FALL

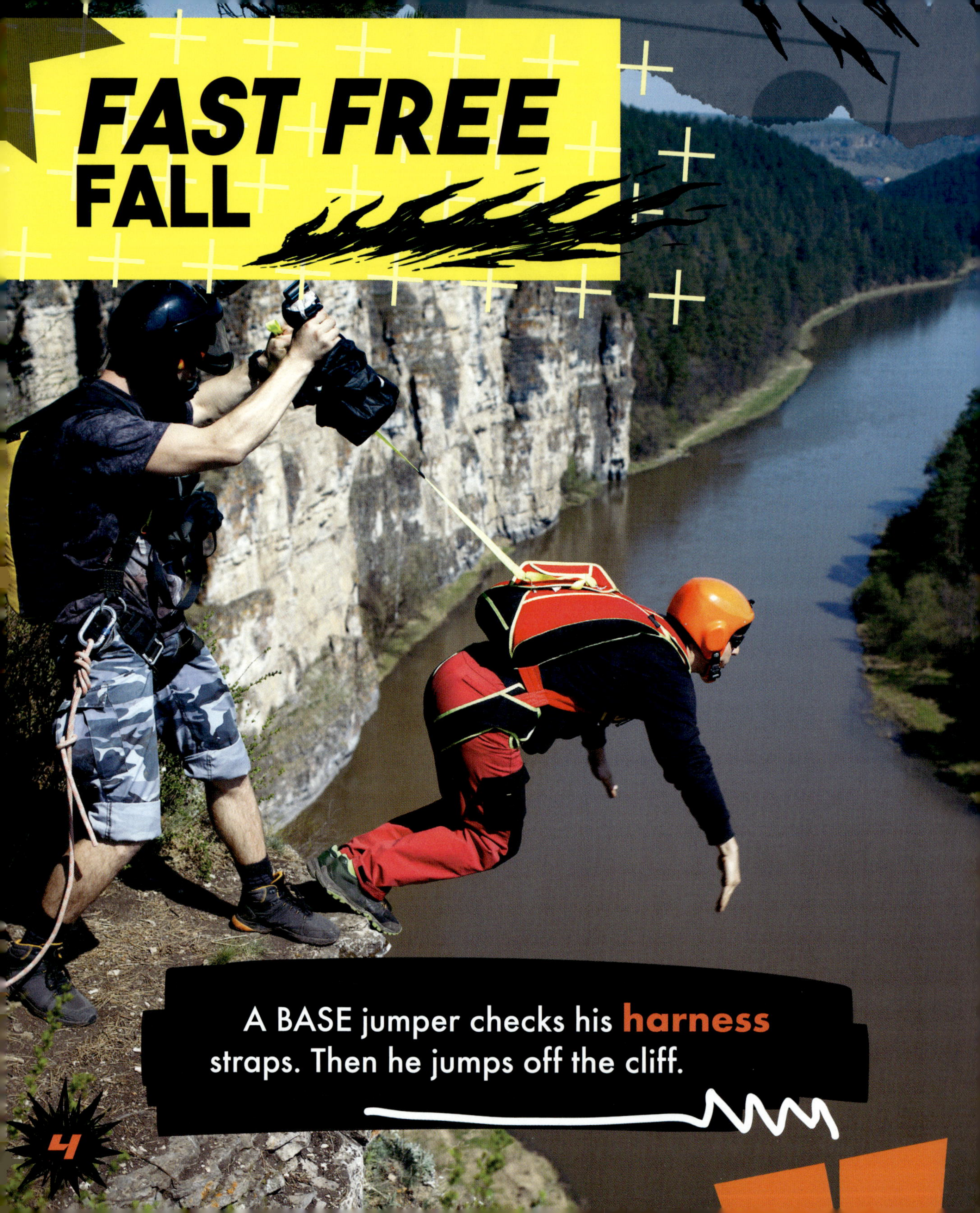

A BASE jumper checks his **harness** straps. Then he jumps off the cliff.

The **free fall** is a heart-pounding rush! It lasts only seconds. The jumper throws open the **parachute** and aims for the landing zone.

WHAT IS BASE JUMPING?

BASE jumping is an extreme sport where people jump off fixed objects. The letters in BASE stand for the different **exit points**.

B is building. A is **antennas**.
S means spans, or bridges. E is earth, like cliffs.

FAMOUS LOCATION

PERRINE BRIDGE

LOCATION	Twin Falls, Idaho, United States
FAMOUS FOR	A bridge 486 feet (148 meters) tall that is a popular spot for first-time BASE jumpers

BASE jumpers use a special **rig**. It holds a parachute that **deploys** quickly.

BASE JUMPING GEAR

Safety gear protects jumpers from rough landings. They wear elbow and knee pads, gloves, and helmets. Some jumpers wear either jumpsuits or **wingsuits**.

THE HISTORY OF BASE JUMPING

The first public parachute jump took place in 1783. In 1912, Frederick Law jumped off the Statue of Liberty.

In 1966, two friends jumped from El Capitan in Yosemite National Park.

EL CAPITAN, YOSEMITE NATIONAL PARK

NEVER TOO OLD

The oldest person to ever BASE jump was 84 years old.

Carl Boenish led a group of skydivers off El Capitan in 1978. He filmed their jump.

Boenish came up with the name BASE jumping. Other skydivers started doing it.

FAMOUS FACE

VALERY ROZOV

BIRTHDAY	December 26, 1964
HOMETOWN	Nizhny Novgorod, Russia
FAMOUS FOR	Completed the highest BASE jump in the world when he jumped 25,262 feet (7,700 meters) off Mount Cho Oyu in the Himalayas

MOUNT CHO OYU

TIMELINE

1783 The first public parachute jump from a building takes place

1912 Frederick Law jumps off the Statue of Liberty

1978 Carl Boenish leads a group of skydivers off El Capitan

1997 BASE jumpers begin to use wingsuits

2008 BASE jumping events are held in Spain and Norway

At first, BASE jumpers used skydiving gear. BASE jumping now uses smaller parachutes that open quickly.

Some BASE jumpers began using wingsuits in 1997. In 2008, BASE jumping events were held in Spain and Norway.

2008 JUMP AT KJERAG, NORWAY

BASE JUMPING TODAY

BASE jumping is dangerous. It requires proper training. Jumpers should become skilled skydivers first.

ONLY ONE

BASE jumping rigs do not have a backup parachute. Jumpers do not have time to use a backup.

It is against the law to BASE jump in many places. In other places, people must have a **permit** to jump.

Perrine Bridge in Idaho allows BASE jumping all year. Beginners like its wide-open landing area.

NEW RIVER GORGE BRIDGE DAY, WEST VIRGINIA

Bridge Day in West Virginia draws hundreds of jumpers. It is the largest BASE jumping event in the world.

HOW TO

BARREL ROLL

1. Jump straight out with body flat
2. Turn onto back
3. Toss parachute
4. Swing arm up and around
5. Turn onto stomach
6. Open parachute

HIGH SPEED

Wingsuit BASE jumpers reach high speeds. The fastest recorded speed is 215 miles (346 kilometers) per hour.

Wingsuit flyers **compete** at the World BASE Race in Norway. The fastest flyer wins!

Some BASE jumpers add other sports. They ski, snowboard, or rock climb into their jumps. They keep pushing their skills higher!

GLOSSARY

antennas—long, metal devices that send out signals

compete—to work for something for which another person is also working

deploys—opens up

exit points—the fixed places that people jump off when BASE jumping

free fall—the time between a jump and when the parachute opens

harness—the straps attached to a parachute backpack

parachute—a device made of fabric that catches air to slow a fall

permit—written permission to do something

rig—a parachute system used to BASE jump

wingsuits—special jumpsuits that let a person glide in the air

TO LEARN MORE

AT THE LIBRARY

Doeden, Matt. *BASE Jumping*. Mankato, Minn.: Black Rabbit Books, 2024.

Grack, Rachel. *Kitesurfing*. Minneapolis, Minn.: Bellwether Media, 2026.

Savon, Eric Raymond. *BASE Jumping*. Mankato, Minn.: Creative Education and Creative Paperbacks, 2025.

ON THE WEB

FACTSURFER

Factsurfer.com gives you a safe, fun way to find more information.

1. Go to www.factsurfer.com.
2. Enter "BASE jumping" into the search box and click 🔍.
3. Select your book cover to see a list of related content.

INDEX

The images in this book are reproduced through the courtesy of: Lukasz Janyst, front cover, p. 1; Vasily Smirnov, front cover, p. 1; shaifulzamri, front cover, pp. 1, 8; Flying Pig Studios, front cover, pp. 1, 16 (inset); sergeyonas, p. 2; Talent for Adventure, p. 3; esalienko, pp. 4, 5, 6, 8 (rig, parachute); Charles Knowles, p. 7 (left); Jorie McBride/ Alamy Stock Photo, p. 7 (right); Salienko Evgenii, p. 8 (inset); cwhy25, p. 8 (helmet); Evgeniya Moroz, p. 9; Rick Neves, pp. 9 (pads), 16; Ambartsumian, p. 9 (gloves); sindret, p. 9 (wingsuit); Anonymous/ Wikimedia Commons, p. 10 (inset); Romanet & Cie/ Wikimedia Commons, p. 10; DrewDuzz, p. 11; Grunertrond/ Wikimedia Commons, p. 12; Lydia Tokareva/ Wikimedia Commons, p. 13 (left); Christophe Diesel Michot/ Alamy Stock Photo, pp. 13 (right), 20 (inset); Daniel Prudek, p. 13 (bottom); Xanthippe26/ Wikimedia Commons, p. 14 (1912); Alex, p. 14 (1997); hakonthingstad/ Flickr, p. 15 (all); Amir Khalid, p. 17; Jeremy Markovich/ Wikimedia Commons, p. 18 (all); Connect Images/ Alamy Stock Photo, p. 20; Cavan Images/ Alamy Stock Photo, p. 21 (all).